Mediterranean Diet Slow Cooker Cookbook

Mediterranean Diet Slow Cooker Cookbook

300-Day For Busy or Lazy Food Lovers Who Want to Save Time, Cook Food
Slowly, and Reduce Their Extra Body Weight.

Addivos Ayamili

TABLE OF CONTENTS

INTRODUCTION

The Mediterranean diet is a healthier diet when it is cooked into a slow cooker. The slow cooker is one of the greatest innovations to cook your food with a healthy cooking style. Using the slow cooking method you can cook your food without losing flavors and the nutritional values of the food. It is one of the most popular cooking methods for those people who want to enjoy the benefits of plant-based foods.

The Mediterranean diet is one of the best scientifically proven diet plan comes with various health benefits. The peoples follow the Mediterranean diet found that decrease the risk of heart-related disease, reduce their extra body weight, control blood sugar levels, and reduce stress and depression.

This book contains 80 well-prepared healthy and delicious Mediterranean diet slow cooker recipes that come from different categories like poultry, meat, beans, grains, soups, stews, and vegetables. The recipes written in this cookbook are unique and written in an easily understandable format. All the recipes start with their preparation and exact cooking time followed by step-by-step cooking instructions. The nutritional value information is written at the end of each recipe. The nutritional information will help to keep track of daily calorie intake. There are lots of books available in the market on this topic thanks for choosing my cookbook. I hope you love and enjoy all the Mediterranean diet slow cooker recipes written in this cookbook.

CHAPTER 1: WHAT IS THE MEDITERRANEAN DIET?

The Mediterranean is a healthy eating habit, pattern, and cooking method developed by the people who live around the coastal area of the Mediterranean Sea. The Mediterranean coastal area is surrounded by 22 countries. Each country has its distinct cuisine and cooking style. These countries are France, Greece, Italy, Spain, Turkey, etc.

The Mediterranean allows you to eat seasonable fruits, vegetables, seafood, beans, whole grains, fish, healthy fats like olive oil, herbs, and spices are used to add flavors and seasoning your foods. The diet avoids highly processed foods, processed meat, and artificial sweeteners. The Mediterranean mainly focuses to eat seasonable and locally available foods which are high in fiber, minerals, nutrients, vitamins, and also having antioxidant properties. The Mediterranean diet is a rich fat diet because about 40% of calories come from fat. The fish includes in the Mediterranean diet is rich in Omega-3 fatty acids. The diet helps to improve heart health, reduce the risk of stroke, help control type-2 diabetes and also reduce the risk of cancers.

The Science Behind the Mediterranean Diet

The Mediterranean diet is a modern nutritional diet plan inspired by traditional dietary patterns that come from the countries situated surrounding of Mediterranean Sea.

The research and study conducted over the Mediterranean diet show that the diet is reducing the risk of cardiovascular diseases. The study conducted over 2600 women over 12 years found that a 25% less risk of developing cardiovascular disease.

The 15 years long research and study over the Mediterranean diet published in JAMA international medicine found that the persons who eat refined carbs having a 38% greater risk of dying from heart-related diseases. According to the American Heart Association, the limit of added sugar into your daily Mediterranean diet is 36 grams for men and 25 grams for women.

Olive oil is used as the main fat during the Mediterranean diet. It is one of the best sources of monounsaturated fats to improve your insulin sensitivity and control your blood sugar level. If you don't have diabetes it also helps to reduce the risk of developing diabetes. Some of the research and studies also state that women who follow the Mediterranean diet have a lower risk of breast and stomach cancer.

What to Eat on the Mediterranean Diet?

The Mediterranean diet is based on easily available seasonable fruits, vegetables, and other ingredients found around the coastal region of the Mediterranean Sea. These ingredients include fresh fruits, vegetables, healthy fats, whole grains, fish, seeds, and nuts. It is one of the good sources of fibers, vitamins, protein, minerals, and antioxidants.

Fruits and Vegetables: Most of the Mediterranean diet part is depending upon seasonable fruits and vegetables. The diet allows you to consume 7 to 10 servings of fresh fruits and vegetables.

- **List of recommended fruits and vegetables:** Apple, grapes, pears, bananas, peaches, figs, melons, dates, strawberries, oranges, tomatoes, spinach, broccoli, cauliflower, sprouts, kale, Brussels, carrot, peas, garlic, leafy green, artichokes, beets, bell peppers, green beans, olives, squash, etc.

Nuts and seeds: Nuts and seeds are a great source of unsaturated fatty acids, fibers, protein, minerals and also have antioxidant properties. It was also a good source of vitamin E, copper, magnesium, and plant sterols.

- **List of recommended nuts and seeds:** Almonds, cashew, walnuts, hazelnuts, pine nuts, macadamia nuts, pistachios, chestnuts, pumpkin seeds, sunflower seeds, sesame seeds, flax seeds, etc.

Whole grains: Whole grains are important parts of a healthy diet. They are present in the whole form of flour with all parts of the seeds like germ, bran, and endosperm. Whole grains are a good source of vitamins, minerals, protein, copper, iron, zinc, and antioxidants.

- **List of recommended whole grains:** Brown rice, whole oats, corn, whole wheat, rye, brown rice, buckwheat, pasta, whole grain bread, bulgur, barley, couscous, quinoa, etc.

Fish and seafood: Fish and seafood are the most popular food that comes under this category. These foods are a good source of protein and omega-3 fatty acids. The omega-3 fatty acids are polyunsaturated fatty acids that reduce the risk of heart disease, improves eye health, fight depression and anxiety.

- **List of fish and seafood:** Tuna, salmon, cod, Pollock, clams, herring, mackerel, shad and flounder, sardine, trout, shrimp, oyster, octopus, tilapia, crab, eel, squid, abalone, mussels, etc.

Meat and Poultry: The moderate portion of red meat and poultry are allowed during the diet period. Meat and poultry are good sources of protein and are also loaded with iodine, vitamins B12, zinc, iron, and fatty acids.

- **List of meat and poultry:** Chicken, turkey, duck, goose, goat, lamb, beef, pork, etc.

Legumes: Legumes are a good source of protein, iron, fiber, folate, magnesium, and potassium. It also comes with antioxidant properties which help to slow down the aging process.

- **List of legumes:** Pulses, kidney beans, chickpeas, lentils, peas, peanuts, pinto beans, white beans, hummus, black beans, etc.

Herbs and Spices: Herbs and spices are used to add taste and flavors to your meal. It also contains phytonutrients that have antioxidant properties and helps to prevent body cell damage.

- **List of Herbs and spices:** Basil, garlic, mint, rosemary, sage, cinnamon, pepper, nutmeg, parsley, bay leaves, cilantro, oregano, etc.

Healthy fats and oil: Olive is taken as the main crop in Mediterranean country so olive oil is used as the main fat in every Mediterranean kitchen. Olive oil is rich in monounsaturated fatty acids which protect you from heart-related disease. The healthy fatty acids in the oil help to increase the HDL (good cholesterol) and decrease the LDL (bad cholesterol) level.

- **List healthy fats and oils:** Olive oil, extra virgin olive oil, avocado oil, olives, and walnut oils, etc.

Dairy: Dairy products are used moderately during the Mediterranean diet because they are high in fats. Add yogurt into your diet it keeps your heart healthy and bone strong.

- **List of dairy:** Yogurt, greek yogurt, cheese, and skim milk.

Food to Avoid During the Mediterranean Diet

Highly Processed Foods: Highly processed foods are low in nutrition and high in calories. These foods contain preservatives which make these foods high in sugar, salt, carbohydrates, and saturated fats.

- **List of highly processed foods:** Energy drink, artificial sweetener, candies, ready meal, white bread, sugary snacks, fizzy drinks, etc.

Processed Meats: Processed meats contain unhealthy saturated fats. It is avoided during the Mediterranean diet. You can consume a moderate amount of unprocessed meat in the Mediterranean diet.

- **List of processed meats:** Bacon, hot dogs, ham, etc.

Trans Fat and Refined oils: Trans fat and refined oils are unhealthy fats responsible to increase bad cholesterol levels. Consumption of these fats leads to obesity, heart-related disease, diabetes, and immune dysfunction.

- **List of trans fat and refined oils:** Vegetable oils, soybean oil, canola oil, cottonseed oil, margarine, spreads, etc.

Benefits of the Mediterranean Diet

The Mediterranean diet promotes eating healthy fresh seasonable fruits and vegetables packed full of nutrients along with some regular exercise. Regular exercise with a Mediterranean diet helps to achieve your goal, also keep you fit and healthy.

1.Reduce the risk of gestational diabetes

The study published in the journal PLOS Medicine on 23 July 2019 was conducted on healthier pregnancy. The researcher's team founded that the Mediterranean diet helps to reduce the risk of gestational diabetes as well as they noted that the reduction of excess weight gain during pregnancy time.

2.Longevity

The food consumed during the Mediterranean diet is healthy and nutritious and also comes with antioxidant properties. Food with antioxidants helps to reduce your oxidative stress level. It helps to prevent the cell damage process and slow down your aging process. The olive oil used in the Mediterranean diet is a good source of monounsaturated fats which helps to prevent heart disease, control blood sugar levels, reduce the risk of inflammatory disease, and increases your lifespan.

3.Reduce stress and depression

The food consumed during the Mediterranean diet is full of antioxidants. It prevents the stress-related cell damage process and improves your mood. Most of the research and study shows that the food with antioxidant properties helps to reduce the stress level and lower the risk of depression.

4.Promote weight loss

The Mediterranean diet allows you to consume fresh green seasonable fruits and vegetables. These foods are healthy unprocessed and low in calories. A daily exercise with a Mediterranean diet will help you to reduce your extra body weight and gives you long-term weight loss benefits.

5.Reduce the risk of cancer

The research and study over the Mediterranean diet show that the diet helps to prevent some types of cancers like breast cancer, colon cancer, and uterine cancer by boosting your immunity process.

CHAPTER 2: POULTRY

Roasted Pepper Greek Chicken

Preparation Time: 10 minutes   Cooking Time: 3 hours   Serve: 4

Ingredients:

- 2 lbs chicken breasts, boneless & skinless
- 1 tsp dried thyme
- 1 tsp dried oregano
- 1 tsp honey
- 1 tbsp garlic, minced
- 3 tbsp red wine vinegar
- 1 medium onion, sliced
- 1 tbsp olive oil
- 1 cup olives, drained
- 12 oz can roasted red peppers, drained & chopped
- Pepper
- Salt

Directions:

1. Heat oil in a pan over high heat.
2. Season chicken with pepper and salt and place into the pan and cook until brown from all the sides.
3. Place chicken in slow cooker. Pour remaining ingredients over chicken.
4. Cover and cook on high for 3 hours.
5. Stir well and serve.

Nutritional Value (Amount per Serving):

- Calories 523
- Fat 24 g
- Carbohydrates 7 g
- Sugar 2 g
- Protein 66 g
- Cholesterol 202 mg

Hearty Chicken with Olives

Preparation Time: 10 minutes   Cooking Time: 4 hours   Serve: 4

Ingredients:

- 4 medium chicken breasts, boneless & skinless
- 2 tbsp capers
- 1 cup roasted red peppers, chopped
- 1 cup kalamata olives
- 1 medium onion, chopped
- 1 tbsp olive oil
- 1 tbsp garlic, minced
- 2 tbsp lemon juice
- 3 tsp Italian seasoning
- Pepper
- Salt

Directions:

1. Heat oil in a pan over high heat.
2. Season chicken with pepper and salt and place into the pan and cook until brown from all the sides.
3. Place chicken in slow cooker. Pour remaining ingredients over chicken.
4. Cover and cook on low for 4 hours.
5. Stir well and serve.

Nutritional Value (Amount per Serving):

- Calories 386
- Fat 19 g
- Carbohydrates 8 g
- Sugar 3 g
- Protein 43 g
- Cholesterol 132 mg

Chicken with Chickpeas & Tomatoes

Preparation Time: 10 minutes   Cooking Time: 4 hours   Serve: 4

Ingredients:

- 2 lbs chicken breasts
- 1 tsp chili powder
- 1 tsp cumin
- 1 tsp oregano
- 1 tsp paprika
- ½ cup chicken broth
- ¼ cup fresh lemon juice
- 2 garlic cloves, minced
- 16 oz tomatoes, chopped
- 30 oz can chickpeas, drained & rinsed
- Salt

Directions:

1. Place chicken into the slow cooker.
2. Pour remaining ingredients over chicken.
3. Cover and cook on low for 4 hours.
4. Stir well and serve.

Nutritional Value (Amount per Serving):

- Calories 722
- Fat 20 g
- Carbohydrates 54 g
- Sugar 3 g
- Protein 78 g
- Cholesterol 202 mg

Hearty Chicken Shawarma

Preparation Time: 10 minutes   Cooking Time: 3 hours   Serve: 4

Ingredients:

- 1 ¼ lbs chicken thighs, skinless & boneless
- ¼ tsp coriander
- ¼ tsp cinnamon
- ½ tsp curry powder
- 1 tsp dried parsley
- 1 tsp paprika
- 1 tsp garlic powder
- 1 ½ tsp cumin
- 2 tbsp garlic, minced
- 3 tbsp olive oil
- ½ cup Greek yogurt
- ¼ cup chicken broth
- ¼ cup fresh lemon juice
- Pepper
- Salt

Directions:

1. Place chicken thighs into the slow cooker.
2. Pour remaining ingredients over chicken thighs.
3. Cover and cook on high for 3 hours.
4. Stir well and serve with brown rice.

Nutritional Value (Amount per Serving):

- Calories 380
- Fat 21 g
- Carbohydrates 3 g
- Sugar 0.7 g
- Protein 42 g
- Cholesterol 126 mg

Parmesan Chicken & Potatoes

Preparation Time: 10 minutes   Cooking Time: 4 hours   Serve: 4

Ingredients:

- 4 chicken thighs, bone-in & skin-on
- 1 cup parmesan cheese, shredded
- 1 lb baby potatoes, halved
- 3 tbsp olive oil
- 4 garlic cloves, minced
- 1 tsp paprika
- 1 tsp pepper
- 1 tsp garlic salt

Directions:

1. Heat 1 tablespoon of oil in a pan over high heat.
2. Season chicken with pepper and salt and place into the pan and cook until brown from all the sides.
3. Place chicken in slow cooker. Pour remaining ingredients except parmesan cheese over chicken.
4. Cover and cook on high for 4 hours.
5. Sprinkle with parmesan cheese and serve.

Nutritional Value (Amount per Serving):

- Calories 443
- Fat 21 g
- Carbohydrates 16 g
- Sugar 0.6 g
- Protein 45 g
- Cholesterol 130 mg

Delicious Chicken Ratatouille

Preparation Time: 10 minutes   Cooking Time: 6 hours   Serve: 4

Ingredients:

- 4 chicken breasts, boneless
- 4 fresh basil leaves
- ¼ cup tomato puree
- ½ tsp dried garlic, minced
- ½ tsp dried oregano
- 16 oz passata
- 1 zucchini, sliced
- 1 eggplant, diced
- 1 yellow pepper, diced
- 1 red pepper, diced
- 1 onion, diced
- Pepper
- Salt

Directions:

1. Place chicken breasts into the slow cooker.
2. Pour remaining ingredients over chicken.
3. Cover and cook on low for 6 hours.
4. Stir well and serve.

Nutritional Value (Amount per Serving):

- Calories 393
- Fat 11 g
- Carbohydrates 24 g
- Sugar 7 g
- Protein 46 g
- Cholesterol 130 mg

Juicy Chicken Gyros

Preparation Time: 10 minutes   Cooking Time: 3 hours   Serve: 4

Ingredients:

- 2 lbs chicken thighs, boneless & skinless
- 1 tsp garlic, minced
- 1 tbsp fresh thyme, chopped
- 1 tbsp fresh basil, chopped
- 2 tbsp fresh oregano, chopped
- 1 lemon juice
- 4 carrots, peeled & chopped
- 1 medium onion, sliced
- Pepper
- Salt

Directions:

1. Add chicken, garlic, thyme, basil, oregano, lemon juice, pepper, and salt into the zip-lock bag. Seal bag and place in refrigerator for overnight.
2. Add carrots and onion into the slow cooker.
3. Pour marinated chicken over carrots and onion.
4. Cover and cook on high for 3 hours.
5. Shred chicken using a fork and serve.

Nutritional Value (Amount per Serving):

- Calories 477
- Fat 17 g
- Carbohydrates 10 g
- Sugar 4 g
- Protein 66 g
- Cholesterol 202 mg

Lemon Chicken

Preparation Time: 10 minutes   Cooking Time: 4 hours   Serve: 4

Ingredients:

- 4 chicken breasts, boneless & skinless
- 3 tbsp parsley, chopped
- 1 cup chicken stock
- 1 tbsp lemon zest
- ¼ cup fresh lemon juice
- 3 tsp dried oregano
- 3 tsp dried rosemary
- 4 garlic cloves, minced
- 1 tsp kosher salt

Directions:

1. Place chicken into the slow cooker.
2. Pour remaining ingredients except parsley over chicken.
3. Cover and cook on high for 4 hours.
4. Garnish with parsley and serve.

Nutritional Value (Amount per Serving):

- Calories 296
- Fat 11 g
- Carbohydrates 3.3 g
- Sugar 0.7 g
- Protein 43 g
- Cholesterol 130 mg

Chicken Souvlaki

Preparation Time: 10 minutes   Cooking Time: 3 hours   Serve: 8

Ingredients:

- 1 ½ lbs chicken breasts, boneless & skinless
- 4 bell peppers, sliced
- 3 tbsp Souvlaki seasoning
- 3 tbsp olive oil
- 2 tbsp fresh lemon juice
- Pepper
- Salt

Directions:

1. Cut chicken breasts into the strips.
2. Place chicken into the slow cooker.
3. Pour remaining ingredients over chicken and mix well.
4. Cover and cook on high for 3 hours.
5. Stir well and serve.

Nutritional Value (Amount per Serving):

- Calories 227
- Fat 11 g
- Carbohydrates 4 g
- Sugar 3 g
- Protein 25 g
- Cholesterol 76 mg

Greek Chicken Drumsticks

Preparation Time: 10 minutes   Cooking Time: 2 hours   Serve: 4

Ingredients:

- 10 chicken drumsticks
- 3 tbsp olive oil
- ½ lemon juice
- ½ tsp dried mint
- 2 tsp dried oregano
- 1 tsp garlic, minced
- Pepper
- Salt

Directions:

1. Place chicken drumsticks into the slow cooker.
2. In a small bowl, mix together oil, lemon juice, mint, oregano, garlic, pepper, and salt and pour over chicken drumsticks.
3. Cover and cook on high for 2 hours.
4. Stir well and serve.

Nutritional Value (Amount per Serving):

- Calories 288
- Fat 17 g
- Carbohydrates 0.8 g
- Sugar 0 g
- Protein 31 g
- Cholesterol 101 mg

Chicken with Vegetables

Preparation Time: 10 minutes   Cooking Time: 4 hours   Serve: 6

Ingredients:

- 2 lbs chicken breasts, boneless & skinless
- 6 garlic cloves, pressed
- ½ lemon juice
- ¼ cup feta cheese, crumbled
- 4 oz fresh spinach
- 1 medium onion, sliced
- 2 tbsp Greek seasoning
- 1 cup olives, drained
- 16 oz can whole pepperoncini peppers
- 16 oz can roasted red pepper strips, drained
- Pepper
- Salt

Directions:

1. Season chicken with pepper and salt and place into the slow cooker.
2. Pour remaining ingredients except lemon juice and feta cheese over chicken and mix well.
3. Cover and cook on low for 4 hours.
4. Add lemon juice and crumbled feta cheese and stir well.
5. Serve and enjoy.

Nutritional Value (Amount per Serving):

- Calories 353
- Fat 15 g
- Carbohydrates 4 g
- Sugar 1 g
- Protein 46 g
- Cholesterol 140 mg

Chicken with Cinnamon

Preparation Time: 10 minutes   Cooking Time: 6 hours   Serve: 8

Ingredients:

- 4 lbs chicken thighs
- ½ cup olives, pitted
- 1 cup green olives, pitted
- ½ tsp ground cinnamon
- 1 tbsp dried oregano
- 1 stick cinnamon
- 1 lemon zest
- 1 cup chicken broth
- 28 oz can whole tomatoes, peeled & mashed
- 2 garlic cloves, minced
- 2 tbsp olive oil
- 1 large onion, sliced
- Pepper
- Salt

Directions:

1. Heat oil in a pan over high heat.
2. Season chicken with pepper and salt and place into the pan and cook until brown from all the sides.
3. Place chicken in slow cooker. Pour remaining ingredients except olives over chicken.
4. Cover and cook on low for 6 hours.
5. Add olives and stir well.
6. Serve and enjoy.

Nutritional Value (Amount per Serving):

- Calories 486
- Fat 21 g
- Carbohydrates 3 g
- Sugar 0.9 g
- Protein 66 g
- Cholesterol 202 mg

Creamy Italian Chicken

Preparation Time: 10 minutes   Cooking Time: 4 hours   Serve: 4

Ingredients:

- 6 chicken breasts, boneless & skinless
- ½ cup chicken stock
- 8 oz cream cheese, cut into pieces
- 10.5 oz cream of chicken soup
- 1.4 oz Italian seasoning

Directions:

1. Place chicken into the slow cooker.
2. Pour remaining ingredients over chicken and stir well.
3. Cover and cook on high for 4 hours.
4. Shred chicken using a fork.
5. Stir well and serve.

Nutritional Value (Amount per Serving):

- Calories 711
- Fat 43 g
- Carbohydrates 8 g
- Sugar 1 g
- Protein 69 g
- Cholesterol 270 mg

Creamy Tuscan Chicken

Preparation Time: 10 minutes   Cooking Time: 4 hours   Serve: 4

Ingredients:

- 4 chicken breasts, boneless & skinless
- 5 oz baby spinach
- ½ tsp red pepper flakes, crushed
- 1 ½ tsp Italian seasoning
- ½ cup parmesan cheese, grated
- 6 oz can sun-dried tomatoes, slivered
- 1 tbsp olive oil
- 30 oz can Alfredo sauce
- Pepper
- Salt

Directions:

1. Heat oil in a pan over high heat.
2. Season chicken with pepper and salt and place into the pan and cook until brown from all the sides.
3. Place chicken in slow cooker. Pour remaining ingredients except spinach over chicken.
4. Cover and cook on low for 4 hours.
5. Add spinach and stir well.
6. Serve and enjoy.

Nutritional Value (Amount per Serving):

- Calories 322
- Fat 15 g
- Carbohydrates 1 g
- Sugar 0.3 g
- Protein 43 g
- Cholesterol 131 mg

Herb Chicken & Potatoes

Preparation Time: 10 minutes   Cooking Time: 4 hours   Serve: 4

Ingredients:

- 4 chicken breasts, boneless
- 1 tsp garlic powder
- 1 tbsp Italian seasoning
- 3 tbsp olive oil
- 3 cups potatoes, chopped
- 1 tsp fresh oregano
- 1 tsp fresh thyme
- Pepper
- Salt

Directions:

1. Add chicken, garlic powder, Italian seasoning, oil, potatoes, pepper, and salt into the slow cooker and stir well.
2. Cover and cook on low for 4 hours.
3. Garnish with oregano and thyme.
4. Serve and enjoy.

Nutritional Value (Amount per Serving):

- Calories 460
- Fat 22 g
- Carbohydrates 19 g
- Sugar 1 g
- Protein 44 g
- Cholesterol 132 mg

Apricot Chicken

Preparation Time: 10 minutes   Cooking Time: 6 hours   Serve: 6

Ingredients:

- 2 lbs chicken thighs, boneless & skinless
- 1 cup dried apricots, halved
- 1 cup onion, sliced
- 1 tsp dried thyme
- 4 garlic cloves, minced
- 3 tbsp Dijon mustard
- 1 lemon juice
- 1 tsp olive oil
- 1 lemon zest
- 1 cup chicken broth
- Pepper
- Salt

Directions:

1. Heat oil in a pan over high heat.
2. Season chicken with pepper and salt and place into the pan and cook until brown from all the sides.
3. Place chicken in slow cooker. Pour remaining ingredients over chicken.
4. Cover and cook on low for 6 hours.
5. Stir well and serve.

Nutritional Value (Amount per Serving):

- Calories 329
- Fat 12 g
- Carbohydrates 6 g
- Sugar 3 g
- Protein 45 g
- Cholesterol 135 mg

Tender Chicken & Potatoes

Preparation Time: 10 minutes   Cooking Time: 4 hours   Serve: 4

Ingredients:

- 4 chicken breasts, boneless & skinless
- 2 tbsp Italian seasoning
- 2 tbsp olive oil
- 2 cups baby carrots
- 1 lb baby potatoes, cubed
- 1 cup chicken stock
- Pepper
- Salt

Directions:

1. Place chicken breasts into the slow cooker.
2. Pour remaining ingredients over chicken.
3. Cover and on high for 4 hours.
4. Stir well and serve.

Nutritional Value (Amount per Serving):

- Calories 427
- Fat 20 g
- Carbohydrates 15 g
- Sugar 0.8 g
- Protein 45 g
- Cholesterol 135 mg

Shredded Greek Chicken

Preparation Time: 10 minutes   Cooking Time: 4 hours   Serve: 6

Ingredients:

- 3 lbs chicken breasts, boneless
- ½ tsp red pepper flakes, crushed
- ½ tsp onion powder
- 1 tsp dried parsley
- 1 tsp dried basil
- 1 tsp dried oregano
- 1 tsp garlic powder
- 12 sun-dried tomatoes, diced
- ½ cup coconut milk
- 1 cup chicken stock
- Pepper
- Salt

Directions:

1. Place chicken breasts into the slow cooker.
2. Pour remaining ingredients over chicken.
3. Cover and cook on high for 4 hours.
4. Shred chicken using a fork.
5. Stir well and serve.

Nutritional Value (Amount per Serving):

- Calories 526
- Fat 22 g
- Carbohydrates 11 g
- Sugar 7 g
- Protein 68 g
- Cholesterol 202 mg

Simple Italian Chicken

Preparation Time: 10 minutes   Cooking Time: 8 hours   Serve: 6

Ingredients:

- 2 lbs chicken breasts, boneless & skinless
- 1 oz Italian salad dressing mix
- 12 oz can pepper rings

Directions:

1. Place chicken into the slow cooker.
2. Pour pepper rings and Italian salad dressing mix over chicken.
3. Cover and cook on low for 8 hours.
4. Stir well and serve.

Nutritional Value (Amount per Serving):

- Calories 301
- Fat 11 g
- Carbohydrates 3 g
- Sugar 0 g
- Protein 43 g
- Cholesterol 135 mg

Sausage & Peppers

Preparation Time: 10 minutes   Cooking Time: 3 hours   Serve: 6

Ingredients:

- 2 lbs Italian sausage links, sliced
- 1 tbsp fresh parsley, chopped
- 2 cups marinara sauce
- ¼ tsp red chili flakes
- 1 tsp Italian seasoning
- 2 garlic cloves, minced
- 1 large onion, sliced
- 1 yellow bell pepper, sliced
- 1 red bell pepper, sliced
- 1 green bell pepper, sliced
- Pepper
- Salt

Directions:

1. Add sausage and remaining ingredients except parsley into the slow cooker and stir well.
2. Cover and cook on high for 3 hours.
3. Garnish with parsley and serve.

Nutritional Value (Amount per Serving):

- Calories 106
- Fat 2 g
- Carbohydrates 18 g
- Sugar 11 g
- Protein 2 g
Cholesterol 2 mg

CHAPTER 3: LAMB, BEEF & PORK

Beef with Artichokes

Preparation Time: 10 minutes   Cooking Time: 7 hours   Serve: 6

Ingredients:

- 2 lbs stewing beef
- 14 oz can artichoke hearts, drained & halved
- 1 bay leaf
- ½ tsp ground cumin
- 1 tsp dried basil
- 1 tsp dried parsley
- 1 tsp dried oregano
- ½ cup olives, pitted & chopped
- 14.5 oz can tomatoes, diced
- 15 oz can tomato sauce
- 4 cups beef broth
- 1 tbsp olive oil
- 4 garlic cloves, chopped
- 1 onion, diced
- Pepper
- Salt

Directions:

1. Heat oil in a pan over medium-high heat.
2. Add meat to the pan and cook until browned from all the sides.
3. Transfer meat into the slow cooker. Pour remaining ingredients over meat.
4. Cover and cook on low for 7 hours.
5. Stir well and serve.

Nutritional Value (Amount per Serving):

- Calories 402
- Fat 14 g
- Carbohydrates 14 g
- Sugar 7 g
- Protein 52 g
- Cholesterol 135 mg

Balsamic Beef

Ingredients:

- 3 lbs beef chuck roast
- 4 garlic cloves, smashed
- 2 tbsp Worcestershire sauce
- ½ cup balsamic vinegar
- ½ cup beef broth
- Pepper
- Salt

Directions:

1. Place beef chuck roast into the slow cooker.
2. Pour remaining ingredients over meat.
3. Cover and cook on low for 8 hours.
4. Shred the meat using a fork.
5. Stir well and serve.

Nutritional Value (Amount per Serving):

- Calories 839
- Fat 63 g
- Carbohydrates 1.9 g
- Sugar 1.2 g
- Protein 59 g
- Cholesterol 234 mg

Tuscan Beef Casserole

Preparation Time: 10 minutes   Cooking Time: 8 hours   Serve: 4

Ingredients:

- 20 oz lean stewing beef
- 15 oz can cannellini beans
- 2 tbsp balsamic vinegar
- ½ tsp onion powder
- 1 tbsp tomato paste
- 2 fresh thyme sprigs
- 1 ½ cups beef stock
- 14 oz can tomatoes, diced
- 4 mushrooms, sliced
- 2 large carrots, chopped
- 2 celery sticks, chopped
- 4 garlic cloves, crushed
- 1 large onion, chopped
- Pepper
- Salt

Directions:

1. Add meat into the slow cooker.
2. Pour remaining ingredients over meat and stir well.
3. Cover and cook on low for 8 hours.
4. Stir well and serve.

Nutritional Value (Amount per Serving):

- Calories 334
- Fat 8 g
- Carbohydrates 14 g
- Sugar 7 g
- Protein 49 g
- Cholesterol 0 mg

Lamb Ragu

Preparation Time: 10 minutes   Cooking Time: 8 hours   Serve: 6

Ingredients:

- 1 ½ lbs lamb shoulder, cut into half
- 2 fresh rosemary sprigs
- 2 bay leaves
- 1 tbsp tomato paste
- ¼ cup beef stock
- 28 oz can tomatoes, crushed
- 1 large onion, diced
- 1 tsp olive oil
- 2 tbsp garlic, minced
- Pepper
- Salt

Directions:

1. Heat oil in a pan over medium heat.
2. Add meat to the pan and cook until browned from all the sides.
3. Transfer meat into the slow cooker. Pour remaining ingredients over meat and stir well.
4. Cover and cook on low for 8 hours.
5. Stir well and serve.

Nutritional Value (Amount per Serving):

- Calories 263
- Fat 9 g
- Carbohydrates 10.5 g
- Sugar 5 g
- Protein 33 g
- Cholesterol 102 mg

Leg of Lamb

Preparation Time: 10 minutes   Cooking Time: 6 hours   Serve: 12

Ingredients:

- 4 lbs leg of lamb
- 2 cups beef stock
- 1 onion, sliced
- 3 tbsp olive oil
- 1 tsp dried mint
- 2 tsp thyme
- 4 garlic cloves, chopped
- Pepper
- Salt

Directions:

1. Place leg of lamb into the slow cooker.
2. Pour remaining ingredients over meat.
3. Cover and cook on low for 6 hours.
4. Shred the meat using a fork and serve.

Nutritional Value (Amount per Serving):

- Calories 320
- Fat 14 g
- Carbohydrates 1 g
- Sugar 0.4 g
- Protein 43 g
- Cholesterol 136 mg

Maple Pork Tenderloin

Preparation Time: 10 minutes   Cooking Time: 8 hours   Serve: 6

Ingredients:

- 2 lbs pork tenderloin
- ½ tsp dried thyme, crumbled
- 1 tbsp apple cider vinegar
- 2 tbsp honey
- 4 tbsp Dijon mustard
- 1 tsp garlic, minced
- ¼ cup maple syrup
- Pepper
- Salt

Directions:

1. Season pork tenderloin with pepper and salt and place into the slow cooker.
2. Pour remaining ingredients over pork tenderloin.
3. Cover and cook on low for 8 hours.
4. Slice and serve.

Nutritional Value (Amount per Serving):

- Calories 280
- Fat 5 g
- Carbohydrates 15 g
- Sugar 13 g
- Protein 40 g
- Cholesterol 110 mg

Flavorful Pork Chops

Preparation Time: 10 minutes   Cooking Time: 8 hours   Serve: 6

Ingredients:

- 2 lbs pork chops
- 1 tsp dried rosemary
- 1 tsp black pepper
- 1 tsp dried thyme
- 2 tsp dried parsley
- 2 tbsp dried oregano
- 2 tbsp Dijon mustard
- 2 garlic cloves, minced
- ¼ cup lemon juice
- 1 cup olive oil
- Salt

Directions:

1. Add pork chops and remaining ingredients into the zip-lock bag. Seal bag and place in refrigerator for overnight.
2. Place marinated pork chops and marinade into the slow cooker.
3. Cover and cook on low for 8 hours.
4. Serve and enjoy.

Nutritional Value (Amount per Serving):

- Calories 786
- Fat 71 g
- Carbohydrates 2 g
- Sugar 0.3 g
- Protein 34 g
- Cholesterol 130 mg

Balsamic Pork Tenderloin

Preparation Time: 10 minutes   Cooking Time: 6 hours   Serve: 6

Ingredients:

- 3 lbs pork tenderloin
- ½ cup water
- 1 tbsp cornstarch
- 2 tbsp soy sauce
- ¼ cup balsamic vinegar
- Pepper
- Salt

Directions:

1. Season pork tenderloin with pepper and salt and place into the slow cooker.
2. Mix together remaining ingredients and pour over pork tenderloin.
3. Cover and cook on low for 6 hours.
4. Slice and serve.

Nutritional Value (Amount per Serving):

- Calories 334
- Fat 8 g
- Carbohydrates 1 g
- Sugar 0.1 g
- Protein 59 g
- Cholesterol 166 mg

Pork Loin Roast

Preparation Time: 10 minutes   Cooking Time: 3 hours   Serve: 6

Ingredients:

- 2 ½ lbs pork loin
- 6 fresh thyme sprigs
- 4 fresh rosemary sprigs
- 2 cups chicken broth
- ½ onion, chopped
- 1 bell pepper, chopped
- ½ lb green beans, trimmed
- 1 lb rutabagas, peeled & cut into 1-inch cubes
- 2 tbsp olive oil
- 1 tsp garlic powder
- Pepper
- Salt

Directions:

1. Place pork loin into the slow cooker.
2. Pour remaining ingredients over pork loin.
3. Cover and cook on high for 3 hours.
4. Remove fresh thyme and rosemary sprigs from slow cooker.
5. Stir well and serve.

Nutritional Value (Amount per Serving):

- Calories 561
- Fat 31 g
- Carbohydrates 11 g
- Sugar 6 g
- Protein 55 g
- Cholesterol 151 mg

Greek Beef & Potatoes

Preparation Time: 10 minutes   Cooking Time: 8 hours   Serve: 6

Ingredients:

- 3 lbs beef chuck roast
- 3 large potatoes, peeled & chopped
- 2 tbsp olive oil
- 5 tbsp red wine vinegar
- 0.7 oz Greek dressing mix
- 14.5 oz can stewed tomatoes
- Pepper
- Salt

Directions:

1. Place beef chuck roast into the slow cooker.
2. Pour remaining ingredients over meat.
3. Cover and cook on low for 8 hours.
4. Stir well and serve.

Nutritional Value (Amount per Serving):

- Calories 993
- Fat 68 g
- Carbohydrates 29 g
- Sugar 2 g
- Protein 62 g
- Cholesterol 234 mg

Juicy & Tender Leg of Lamb

Preparation Time: 10 minutes   Cooking Time: 8 hours   Serve: 8

Ingredients:

- 4 lbs leg of lamb, boneless
- 1 cup white wine
- 1 cup chicken broth
- 1 tbsp fresh rosemary, chopped
- 4 garlic cloves, minced
- 2 lbs potatoes, quartered
- 2 tbsp olive oil
- 1 lemon juice
- Pepper
- Salt

Directions:

1. Heat oil in a pan over medium-high heat.
2. Place meat on a hot pan and sear until browned from all the sides.
3. Place meat into the slow cooker. Pour remaining ingredients over meat.
4. Cover and cook on low for 8 hours.
5. Stir well and serve.

Nutritional Value (Amount per Serving):

- Calories 563
- Fat 20 g
- Carbohydrates 19 g
- Sugar 1 g
- Protein 66 g
- Cholesterol 204 mg

Pulled Pork Gyros

Preparation Time: 10 minutes   Cooking Time: 8 hours   Serve: 12

Ingredients:

- 3 ½ lbs pork shoulder, boneless
- ¼ cup Greek spice rub
- 2 tbsp apple cider vinegar
- 1 lemon juice
- ½ cup orange juice

Directions:

1. Place pork shoulder into the slow cooker.
2. Pour remaining ingredients over meat.
3. Cover and cook on low for 8 hours.
4. Shred the meat using a fork and serve.

Nutritional Value (Amount per Serving):

- Calories 390
- Fat 28 g
- Carbohydrates 1 g
- Sugar 0.9 g
- Protein 30 g
- Cholesterol 119 mg

Greek Shredded Pork

Preparation Time: 10 minutes   Cooking Time: 4 hours   Serve: 8

Ingredients:

- 2 lbs pork tenderloin
- 16 oz can pepperoncini peppers, sliced
- 2 tbsp Greek seasoning

Directions:

1. Place pork tenderloin into the slow cooker.
2. Pour pepperoncini pepper and Greek seasoning over pork tenderloin.
3. Cover and cook on high for 4 hours.
4. Shred the meat using a fork and serve.

Nutritional Value (Amount per Serving):

- Calories 167
- Fat 4 g
- Carbohydrates 1 g
- Sugar 0 g
- Protein 29 g
- Cholesterol 83 mg

Easy Lamb Chops

Preparation Time: 10 minutes   Cooking Time: 6 hours   Serve: 4

Ingredients:

- 6 lamb chops
- 1 onion, chopped
- 2 carrots, chopped
- 2 celery sticks, chopped
- 4 cups beef stock
- Pepper
- Salt

Directions:

1. Place lamb chops into the slow cooker.
2. Pour remaining ingredients over lamb chops.
3. Cover and cook on low for 6 hours.
4. Serve and enjoy.

Nutritional Value (Amount per Serving):

- Calories 953
- Fat 36 g
- Carbohydrates 5 g
- Sugar 2 g
- Protein 141 g
- Cholesterol 441 mg

Greek Flank Steak

Preparation Time: 10 minutes   Cooking Time: 8 hours   Serve: 4

Ingredients:

- 1 ¼ lbs flank steaks, cut in half
- 1 cup beef broth
- 1 tbsp dried oregano
- 2 garlic cloves, minced
- 2 tbsp olive oil
- 1 large onion, chopped
- Pepper
- Salt

Directions:

1. Place steaks into the slow cooker.
2. Pour remaining ingredients over steaks.
3. Cover and cook on low for 8 hours.
4. Serve and enjoy.

Nutritional Value (Amount per Serving):

- Calories 365
- Fat 19 g
- Carbohydrates 5 g
- Sugar 1 g
- Protein 41 g
- Cholesterol 78 mg

Olive Feta Beef

Ingredients:

- 2 lbs beef stew meat, cut into half-inch pieces
- 1 cup olives, pitted, and cut in half
- 30 oz can tomatoes, diced
- 1/2 cup feta cheese, crumbled
- Pepper
- Salt

Directions:

1. Add meat into the slow cooker.
2. Pour remaining ingredients over meat.
3. Cover and cook on low for 6 hours.
4. Stir well and serve.

Nutritional Value (Amount per Serving):

- Calories 370
- Fat 14 g
- Carbohydrates 9 g
- Sugar 5 g
- Protein 49 g
- Cholesterol 146 mg

Balsamic Tomato Beef

Preparation Time: 10 minutes   Cooking Time: 6 hours   Serve: 6

Ingredients:

- 2 lbs chuck roast, boneless
- 2 tbsp balsamic vinegar
- 2 tsp herb de Provence
- 1/3 cup sun-dried tomatoes, chopped
- 8 garlic cloves, chopped
- 1/4 cup fresh parsley, chopped
- 1/4 cup olives, chopped
- 1/2 cup chicken stock

Directions:

1. Add meat into the slow cooker.
2. Pour remaining ingredients over the meat.
3. Cover and cook on high for 6 hours.
4. Stir well and serve.

Nutritional Value (Amount per Serving):

- Calories 344
- Fat 13 g
- Carbohydrates 2.3 g
- Sugar 0.4 g
- Protein 50 g
- Cholesterol 153 mg

Herb Beef

Preparation Time: 10 minutes   Cooking Time: 6 hours   Serve: 6

Ingredients:

- 2 lbs stew beef, cut into 1-inch cubes
- 1 tsp dried basil
- 12 oz artichoke hearts, drained
- 1 onion, diced
- 1 tsp dried oregano
- 12 oz roasted red peppers, drained and sliced
- 2 cups marinara sauce

Directions:

1. Add meat and remaining ingredients into the slow cooker and stir well.
2. Cover and cook on low for 6 hours.
3. Stir well and serve.

Nutritional Value (Amount per Serving):

- Calories 343
- Fat 11 g
- Carbohydrates 22 g
- Sugar 11 g
- Protein 37 g
- Cholesterol 2 mg

Balsamic Greek Beef

Preparation Time: 10 minutes   Cooking Time: 8 hours   Serve: 6

Ingredients:

- 2 lbs beef chuck roast
- 1 medium onion, sliced
- 1/4 cup balsamic vinegar
- 1/4 cup dates, pitted and chopped
- 4 shallots, sliced
- 1 cup water
- Pepper
- Salt

Directions:

1. Add meat and remaining ingredients into the slow cooker and stir well.
2. Cover and cook on low for 8 hours.
3. Stir well and serve.

Nutritional Value (Amount per Serving):

- Calories 579
- Fat 42 g
- Carbohydrates 7 g
- Sugar 5 g
- Protein 39 g
- Cholesterol 156 mg

Rosemary Lamb

Preparation Time: 10 minutes   Cooking Time: 8 hours   Serve: 12

Ingredients:

- 4 lbs lamb leg, boneless
- 1 tbsp rosemary, crushed
- 1 tsp black pepper
- 1/4 cup water
- 1/4 cup lemon juice
- 1/4 tsp salt

Directions:

1. Add meat and remaining ingredients into the slow cooker and stir well.
2. Cover and cook on low for 8 hours.
3. Serve and enjoy.

Nutritional Value (Amount per Serving):

- Calories 351
- Fat 25g
- Carbohydrates 0.4 g
- Sugar 0.1 g
- Protein 26 g
- Cholesterol 107 mg

CHAPTER 4: BEANS & GRAINS

Delicious Lima Beans

Preparation Time: 10 minutes   Cooking Time: 8 hours   Serve: 6

Ingredients:

- 1 lb dry lima beans, soaked overnight & drained
- ½ cup olive oil
- 4 cups chicken stock
- 2 bay leaves
- 1 tbsp ground thyme
- 1 tbsp ground oregano
- 28 oz can tomatoes, crushed
- 4 garlic cloves, minced
- 3 celery sticks, diced
- 1 onion, diced
- Pepper
- Salt

Directions:

1. Add beans and remaining ingredients into the slow cooker and stir well.
2. Cover and cook on low for 8 hours.
3. Stir well and serve.

Nutritional Value (Amount per Serving):

- Calories 336
- Fat 17 g
- Carbohydrates 57 g
- Sugar 7 g
- Protein 18 g
- Cholesterol 0 mg

Black Bean Rice

Preparation Time: 10 minutes   **Cooking Time: 3 hours**   **Serve: 6**

Ingredients:

- 1 lb dry black beans, soaked overnight & drained
- 2 tsp chili powder
- 4 tsp ground cumin
- 4 tbsp garlic, minced
- 2 cups brown rice
- 6 cups chicken stock
- Pepper
- Salt

Directions:

1. Add black beans and remaining ingredients into the slow cooker and stir well.
2. Cover and cook on high for 3 hours.
3. Stir well and serve.

Nutritional Value (Amount per Serving):

- Calories 513
- Fat 3 g
- Carbohydrates 99 g
- Sugar 2 g
- Protein 22 g
- Cholesterol 0 mg

White Bean Turkey Chili

Preparation Time: 10 minutes   Cooking Time: 4 hours   Serve: 8

Ingredients:

- 2 lbs ground turkey
- 2 cups chicken broth
- 4.5 oz can green chili, chopped
- 15 oz can pumpkin puree
- 30 oz can northern beans, rinsed & drained
- 1 tsp oregano
- 1 ½ tbsp cumin
- 2 bay leaves
- 1 tsp chili powder
- ½ tsp olive oil
- 1 tbsp garlic, minced
- 1 small onion, chopped
- Pepper
- Salt

Directions:

1. Heat oil in a pan over high heat.
2. Add meat to the pan and cook for 5 minutes.
3. Add garlic and onion and sauté for 3-5 minutes.
4. Transfer the meat mixture and remaining ingredients into the slow cooker and stir well.
5. Cover and cook on high for 4 hours.
6. Stir well and serve.

Nutritional Value (Amount per Serving):

- Calories 244
- Fat 13 g
- Carbohydrates 2 g
- Sugar 0.6 g
- Protein 32 g
- Cholesterol 116 mg

Greek Chickpeas

Ingredients:

- 28 oz can chickpeas, drained & rinsed
- ¼ cup parsley, minced
- 14 oz can tomatoes, diced
- 28 oz can tomatoes, crushed
- ½ tsp red pepper flakes
- 1 ½ tsp dried oregano
- 4 garlic cloves, minced
- 2 tsp olive oil
- 1 large onion, chopped
- Pepper
- Salt

Directions:

1. Heat oil in a large pan over medium heat.
2. Add onion to the pan and sauté for 5 minutes.
3. Add garlic, red pepper flakes, and oregano and cook for a minute.
4. Transfer sautéed onion to the slow cooker. Add remaining ingredients into the slow cooker and stir well.
5. Cover and cook on low for 8 hours.
6. Stir well and serve.

Nutritional Value (Amount per Serving):

- Calories 171
- Fat 2 g
- Carbohydrates 32 g
- Sugar 5 g
- Protein 6 g
- Cholesterol 0 mg

Maple Oatmeal

Preparation Time: 10 minutes   Cooking Time: 6 hours   Serve: 8

Ingredients:

- 2 cups steel-cut oats
- 1 tsp coconut oil, melted
- 1 tsp vanilla
- ¼ cup maple syrup
- 2 tsp cinnamon
- 3 cups milk
- 4 cups water
- ¼ tsp kosher salt

Directions:

1. Add oats and remaining ingredients into the slow cooker and stir well.
2. Cover and cook on low for 6 hours.
3. Stir well and serve.

Nutritional Value (Amount per Serving):

- Calories 239
- Fat 5 g
- Carbohydrates 38 g
- Sugar 10 g
- Protein 9 g
- Cholesterol 8 mg

Sausage & White Beans

Preparation Time: 10 minutes   Cooking Time: 6 hours   Serve: 8

Ingredients:

- 2 cups dry white beans, soaked overnight & drained
- ½ cup water
- 14.5 oz can tomatoes
- 5 turkey sausage links, sliced
- 2 tsp Italian seasoning
- 10 fresh sage leaves
- 4 garlic cloves, minced
- 2 celery stalks, chopped
- Pepper
- Salt

Directions:

1. Add white beans and remaining ingredients into the slow cooker and stir well.
2. Cover and cook on low for 6 hours.
3. Stir well and serve.

Nutritional Value (Amount per Serving):

- Calories 213
- Fat 3 g
- Carbohydrates 33 g
- Sugar 3 g
- Protein 14 g
- Cholesterol 8 mg

Spicy Pinto Beans

Preparation Time: 10 minutes   Cooking Time: 8 hours   Serve: 6

Ingredients:

- 1 lb pinto beans, soaked overnight & drained
- 14.5 oz beef broth
- 4 cups vegetable broth
- 4 bacon slices, cooked & chopped
- 2 jalapeno pepper, chopped
- 15 oz can tomatoes, diced
- 1 tsp garlic powder
- 1 tsp cumin
- 4 garlic cloves, minced
- 1 medium onion, sliced
- Pepper
- Salt

Directions:

1. Add pinto beans and remaining ingredients into the slow cooker and stir well.
2. Cover and cook on high for 8 hours.
3. Stir well and serve.

Nutritional Value (Amount per Serving):

- Calories 329
- Fat 2.4 g
- Carbohydrates 54 g
- Sugar 5 g
- Protein 22 g
- Cholesterol 0 mg

Apple Cinnamon Oatmeal

Preparation Time: 10 minutes   Cooking Time: 6 hours   Serve: 4

Ingredients:

- 1 cup steel-cut oats
- 1 tsp cinnamon
- 1 tsp vanilla
- 1 tbsp maple syrup
- 1 cup apple, chopped
- 2 cups unsweetened almond milk
- 2 cups water
- ¼ tsp salt

Directions:

1. Add oats and remaining ingredients into the slow cooker and stir well.
2. Cover and cook on low for 6 hours.
3. Stir well and serve.

Nutritional Value (Amount per Serving):

- Calories 227
- Fat 4.9 g
- Carbohydrates 39 g
- Sugar 8.9 g
- Protein 6 g
- Cholesterol 0 mg

Barley Risotto

Preparation Time: 10 minutes   Cooking Time: 8 hours   Serve: 8

Ingredients:

- 2 cups barley, rinsed & drained
- 2 tbsp fresh parsley, chopped
- 1 tbsp lemon juice
- 2 cups parmesan cheese, grated
- 1 tbsp thyme, chopped
- 4 garlic cloves, minced
- 4 shallots, sliced
- 10 cups water
- 1 cup mushrooms, sliced
- Pepper
- Salt

Directions:

1. Add barley, parsley, thyme, garlic, shallots, mushrooms, water, pepper, and salt into the slow cooker and stir well.
2. Cover and cook on low for 8 hours.
3. Stir in parmesan cheese and lemon juice.
4. Serve and enjoy.

Nutritional Value (Amount per Serving):

- Calories 169
- Fat 1 g
- Carbohydrates 34 g
- Sugar 0.6 g
- Protein 6.2 g
- Cholesterol 0 mg

Apple Cinnamon Buckwheat Porridge

Preparation Time: 10 minutes   Cooking Time: 4 hours   Serve: 4

Ingredients:

- 1 ½ cups buckwheat grots
- 1 tsp vanilla
- 1 tsp pumpkin pie spice
- 2 tsp cinnamon
- ½ cup maple syrup
- 3 apples, cored & chopped
- 1 cup unsweetened almond milk
- 4 cups water
- Pinch of salt

Directions:

1. Add buckwheat grots and remaining ingredients into the slow cooker and stir well.
2. Cover and cook on high for 4 hours.
3. Stir well and serve.

Nutritional Value (Amount per Serving):

- Calories 426
- Fat 3.5 g
- Carbohydrates 97 g
- Sugar 41 g
- Protein 9 g
- Cholesterol 0 mg

CHAPTER 5: SOUPS & STEWS

Greek Pork Stew

Preparation Time: 10 minutes   Cooking Time: 8 hours 10 minutes   Serve: 4

Ingredients:

- 4 pork chops, boneless
- 1 onion, sliced
- 2 1/4 cups vegetable stock
- 14 oz can tomatoes, chopped
- 1/2 cup olives
- 2 tsp garlic, minced
- 1 tbsp olive oil
- 2 tsp chili, diced
- 1 bay leaf
- 2 yellow bell pepper, sliced
- 2 red bell peppers, sliced

Directions:

1. Heat oil in a pan over medium heat.
2. Add garlic, onion, and chili to the pan and sauté for 5 minutes.
3. Add pork chops to the pan and cook for 5 minutes.
4. Transfer pork chops mixture into the slow cooker along with remaining ingredients and stir well.
5. Cover and cook on low for 8 hours.
6. Stir and serve.

Nutritional Value (Amount per Serving):

- Calories 381
- Fat 25 g
- Carbohydrates 18 g
- Sugar 10 g
- Protein 20 g
- Cholesterol 69 mg

Chickpea Beef Stew

Preparation Time: 10 minutes   Cooking Time: 4 hours   Serve: 4

Ingredients:

- 2 lbs stew beef, cut into cubes
- 10 oz can tomatoes, diced
- 1 carrot, peeled and sliced
- 1 onion, chopped
- 15 oz can chickpeas, drained
- 1/2 cup vegetable stock
- 1/2 tsp dried rosemary, crushed
- Pepper
- Salt

Directions:

1. Add meat and remaining ingredients into the slow cooker and stir well.
2. Cover and cook on low for 4 hours.
3. Stir well and serve.

Nutritional Value (Amount per Serving):

- Calories 491
- Fat 14 g
- Carbohydrates 31 g
- Sugar 4 g
- Protein 56 g
- Cholesterol 0 mg

Chicken Quinoa Stew

Preparation Time: 10 minutes   Cooking Time: 6 hours 40 minutes   Serve: 6

Ingredients:

- 1 1/4 lbs chicken thighs, skinless and boneless
- 1 bay leaf
- 1 garlic clove, chopped
- 1 cup onion, chopped
- 4 cups chicken stock
- 4 cups butternut squash, chopped
- 3/4 cup olives, sliced
- 1/2 cup quinoa, uncooked
- 1/2 tsp ground fennel seeds
- 1 tsp dried oregano
- Pepper
- Kosher salt

Directions:

1. Add chicken, garlic, onion, stock, squash, fennel seeds, oregano, bay leaf, pepper, and salt to the slow cooker and stir well.
2. Cover and cook on low for 6 hours.
3. Remove chicken from the slow cooker and shred using a fork.
4. Add quinoa and stir well. Cover and cook on low for 30 minutes more.
5. Return shredded to the slow cooker along with olives and stir well.
6. Serve and enjoy.

Nutritional Value (Amount per Serving):

- Calories 309
- Fat 10 g
- Carbohydrates 23 g
- Sugar 3.4 g
- Protein 31 g
- Cholesterol 84 mg

Tasty Chicken Stew

Preparation Time: 10 minutes   Cooking Time: 6 hours 25 minutes   Serve: 6

Ingredients:

- 6 chicken thighs, boneless and cut into cubes
- 2 tomatoes, diced
- 2 garlic cloves, minced
- 1 small onion, diced
- 2 celery stalks, sliced
- 2 carrots, peeled and sliced
- 1/2 tsp fennel seeds, crushed
- 2 tbsp white wine
- 1 3/4 cup chicken stock
- 8 baby potatoes, cut in half
- 1 tbsp vinegar
- 1 tbsp cornstarch
- 1/4 cup water
- 1/2 tsp salt

Directions:

1. Add chicken, potatoes, tomatoes, garlic, onion, fennel seeds, wine, tomato paste, stock, celery, carrots, and salt into the slow cooker.
2. Cover and cook on low for 6 hours.
3. In a small bowl, mix together water and cornstarch and pour into a slow cooker.
4. Stir in vinegar. Cook stew on high for 25 minutes more.
5. Serve and enjoy.

Nutritional Value (Amount per Serving):

- Calories 313
- Fat 11 g
- Carbohydrates 6 g
- Sugar 2 g
- Protein 43 g
- Cholesterol 130 mg

Chicken Vegetable Soup

Preparation Time: 10 minutes   Cooking Time: 7 hours   Serve: 4

Ingredients:

- 1 lb chicken breast, skinless and boneless
- 2 garlic cloves, minced
- 1 small zucchini, cubed
- 1 small onion, diced
- 2 celery stalks, diced
- 2 tsp Worcestershire sauce
- 5 cups chicken broth
- 1/4 tsp dried thyme leaves
- 1 bay leaves
- 1 medium carrot, diced
- 1/2 tsp sea salt

Directions:

1. Add all ingredients to the slow cooker and mix well.
2. Cover and cook on low for 7 hours.
3. Shred the chicken using a fork and stir well.
4. Serve and enjoy.

Nutritional Value (Amount per Serving):

- Calories 202
- Fat 4 g
- Carbohydrates 6 g
- Sugar 3.5 g
- Protein 31 g
- Cholesterol 73 mg

Chicken Kale Soup

Preparation Time: 10 minutes   Cooking Time: 7 hours   Serve: 6

Ingredients:

- 6 chicken thighs, skinless and boneless
- 3 garlic cloves, smashed
- 1/2 onion, chopped
- 3 1/2 cups chicken broth
- 1 1/2 tsp parsley
- 3 cups kale, chopped
- 1 cups carrots, shredded
- Pepper
- Salt

Directions:

1. Add chicken, garlic, broth, and onion into the slow cooker and stir well.
2. Cover and cook on low for 6 hours.
3. Remove chicken from the slow cooker and shred using a fork.
4. Return shredded chicken to the slow cooker along with carrots, parsley, and kale and stir well and cook for 1 hour more.
5. Stir well and serve.

Nutritional Value (Amount per Serving):

- Calories 330
- Fat 11 g
- Carbohydrates 7 g
- Sugar 1 g
- Protein 46 g
- Cholesterol 130 mg

Hearty Chicken Chili

Preparation Time: 10 minutes   Cooking Time: 8 hours 15 minutes   Serve: 6

Ingredients:

- 1 1/2 lbs chicken breasts, skinless and boneless
- 2 1/2 tsp ground cumin
- 4 garlic cloves, minced
- 1 jalapeno pepper, seeded and diced
- 1/2 bell pepper, diced
- 1 small onion, diced
- 1/2 cup cilantro, chopped
- 1/2 lime juice
- 14 oz can coconut milk
- 1 tbsp olive oil
- 4 cups chicken stock
- 2 tsp chili powder
- 1 tsp oregano
- Pepper
- Salt

Directions:

1. Add all ingredients except coconut milk, cilantro, and lime juice into the slow cooker and stir well.
2. Cover and cook on low for 8 hours.
3. Add coconut milk and stir well.
4. Cover and cook on low for 15 minutes more.
5. Stir in cilantro and lime juice.
6. Serve and enjoy.

Nutritional Value (Amount per Serving):

- Calories 261
- Fat 11 g
- Carbohydrates 4 g
- Sugar 1 g
- Protein 34 g
- Cholesterol 101 mg

Flavorful Chicken Stew

Preparation Time: 10 minutes   Cooking Time: 4 hours   Serve: 4

Ingredients:

- 28 oz chicken thighs, skinless
- 2 garlic cloves, minced
- 1/2 tsp dried rosemary
- 1/2 onion, diced
- 2 carrots, peeled and diced
- 1 cup celery, diced
- 1/2 cup heavy cream
- 1 cup fresh spinach
- 1/2 tsp oregano
- 1/4 tsp dried thyme
- 2 cups chicken stock
- Pepper
- Salt

Directions:

1. Add all ingredients except cream and spinach into the slow cooker and stir well.
2. Cover and cook on low for 4 hours.
3. Stir in spinach and cream.
4. Stir well and serve.

Nutritional Value (Amount per Serving):

- Calories 461
- Fat 20 g
- Carbohydrates 6 g
- Sugar 2 g
- Protein 59 g
- Cholesterol 197 mg

Tasty Beef Stew

Preparation Time: 10 minutes   Cooking Time: 8 hours 10 minutes   Serve: 6

Ingredients:

- 2 lbs beef stew meat
- 1 small onion, chopped
- 1 tsp Worcestershire sauce
- 1 tsp paprika
- 1 tsp pepper
- 1 tbsp olive oil
- 4 medium celery sticks, sliced
- 3 medium carrots, sliced
- 2 tbsp garlic, minced
- 4 cups beef broth
- 1 1/2 tsp salt

Directions:

1. Heat olive oil in a pan over medium heat.
2. Season meat with pepper and salt and place into the hot pan with onion, and garlic and cook until meat is lightly brown on all sides.
3. Transfer meat mixture to the slow cooker along with remaining ingredients and stir well.
4. Cover and cook on low for 8 hours.
5. Stir well and serve.

Nutritional Value (Amount per Serving):

- Calories 351
- Fat 12 g
- Carbohydrates 6 g
- Sugar 2 g
- Protein 49 g
- Cholesterol 135 mg

Greek Chickpea Soup

Preparation Time: 10 minutes   Cooking Time: 3 hours   Serve: 6

Ingredients:

- 2 cups dry chickpeas, soaked overnight & drained
- 1 cup tomato sauce
- 1 lemon juice
- 2 tbsp dried oregano
- 1/3 cup olive oil
- 2 garlic cloves, minced
- 6 cups chicken stock
- 1 onion, minced
- Pepper
- Salt

Directions:

1. Heat oil in a pan over medium heat.
2. Add onion to the pan and sauté until softened.
3. Transfer sautéed onion and remaining ingredients into the slow cooker and stir well.
4. Cover and cook on high for 3 hours.
5. Stir well and serve.

Nutritional Value (Amount per Serving):

- Calories 372
- Fat 16 g
- Carbohydrates 46 g
- Sugar 10 g
- Protein 14 g
- Cholesterol 0 mg

Healthy Lentil Soup

Preparation Time: 10 minutes   Cooking Time: 8 hours 5 minutes   Serve: 6

Ingredients:

- 1 cup green lentils, rinsed & drained
- 2 tbsp red wine vinegar
- 2 bay leaves
- 2 tbsp tomato paste
- 1 cup tomato sauce
- 5 cups chicken stock
- 1 celery stalk, diced
- 2 carrots, diced
- 2 tbsp olive oil
- 3 garlic cloves, minced
- 1 onion, chopped
- Pepper
- Salt

Directions:

1. Heat oil in a pan over medium heat.
2. Add onion to the pan and sauté for 5 minutes.
3. Transfer sautéed onion and remaining ingredients into the slow cooker and stir well.
4. Cover and cook on low for 8 hours.
5. Stir well and serve.

Nutritional Value (Amount per Serving):

- Calories 195
- Fat 5 g
- Carbohydrates 27 g
- Sugar 5 g
- Protein 10 g
- Cholesterol 0 mg

Tuscan Chicken Stew

Preparation Time: 10 minutes   Cooking Time: 6 hours   Serve: 6

Ingredients:

- 6 chicken thighs, boneless
- 1 rosemary sprig
- 1 tsp ground fennel seeds
- 2 tbsp white wine
- 1 tbsp tomato paste
- 1 ¾ cups chicken stock
- 12 baby potatoes, cut in half
- 2 tomatoes, diced
- 2 garlic cloves, minced
- 1 small onion, diced
- 2 celery stalks, sliced
- 2 carrots, peeled & sliced
- ½ tsp salt

Directions:

1. Add chicken and remaining ingredients into the slow cooker and stir well.
2. Cover and cook on low for 6 hours.
3. Discard the rosemary sprig from a slow cooker and shred the chicken using a fork.
4. Stir well and serve.

Nutritional Value (Amount per Serving):

- Calories 309
- Fat 11 g
- Carbohydrates 6 g
- Sugar 3 g
- Protein 43 g
- Cholesterol 130 mg

Green Lentil Soup

Preparation Time: 10 minutes   Cooking Time: 5 hours   Serve: 6

Ingredients:

- 2 cups green lentils, rinsed & drained
- 1 cup fresh parsley, chopped
- 3 cups baby spinach
- 6 cups vegetable stock
- 1 tsp cumin
- ½ tsp paprika
- 1 tsp turmeric
- 3 tbsp tomato paste
- 2 potatoes, cubed
- 1 bell pepper, diced
- 2 carrots, diced
- 6 garlic cloves, minced
- 1 onion, chopped
- Pepper
- Salt

Directions:

1. Add lentils and remaining ingredients except spinach into the slow cooker and stir well.
2. Cover and cook on low for 5 hours.
3. Add spinach and stir until spinach is wilted.
4. Serve and enjoy.

Nutritional Value (Amount per Serving):

- Calories 318
- Fat 1 g
- Carbohydrates 59 g
- Sugar 6 g
- Protein 19 g
- Cholesterol 0 mg

Flavorful Lentil Soup

Preparation Time: 10 minutes   Cooking Time: 4 hours   Serve: 8

Ingredients:

- 1 ½ cups green lentils, rinsed & drained
- 9 cups vegetable broth
- 2 bay leaves
- 3 tbsp soy sauce
- 1 tsp thyme
- 2 tsp oregano
- 1 tbsp garlic powder
- 2 cups corn
- 4 cups potatoes, diced
- 3 carrots, diced
- 3 celery stalks, diced
- 2 medium onions, diced
- Pepper
- Salt

Directions:

1. Add green lentils and remaining ingredients into the slow cooker and stir well.
2. Cover and cook on high for 4 hours.
3. Stir well and serve.

Nutritional Value (Amount per Serving):

- Calories 285
- Fat 2 g
- Carbohydrates 48 g
- Sugar 6 g
- Protein 18 g
- Cholesterol 0 mg

White Bean Soup

Preparation Time: 10 minutes   Cooking Time: 8 hours   Serve: 4

Ingredients:

- 45 oz can white beans, rinsed & drained
- 1 tsp dried oregano
- 1 bay leaf
- ½ tsp dried rosemary
- 32 oz vegetable stock
- 2 tsp garlic, minced
- 1 cup carrots, chopped
- ½ tsp dried thyme
- 1 cup onion, chopped
- 1 cup celery, chopped
- 1 tsp dried basil
- Pepper
- Salt

Directions:

1. Add white beans and remaining ingredients into the slow cooker and stir well.
2. Cover and cook on low for 8 hours.
3. Stir well and serve.

Nutritional Value (Amount per Serving):

- Calories 277
- Fat 2 g
- Carbohydrates 48 g
- Sugar 4 g
- Protein 15 g
- Cholesterol 0 mg

Chickpea Stew

Ingredients:

- 1 ½ lbs ground turkey
- 2 tbsp parsley, chopped
- 2 bay leaves
- ½ tsp red pepper flakes, crushed
- 1 tsp coriander
- 2 tsp paprika
- 2 tsp turmeric
- 2 cups chicken broth
- 30 oz can chickpeas, drained
- 28 oz can tomatoes, diced
- 1 cup celery, diced
- 1 cup carrots, diced
- 3 tbsp poblano pepper, chopped
- 1 tbsp olive oil
- 2 garlic cloves, chopped
- 1 onion, chopped
- Pepper
- Salt

Directions:

1. Heat oil in a pan over medium-high heat.
2. Add meat to the pan and cook for 10-12 minutes.
3. Transfer meat and remaining ingredients into the slow cooker and stir well.
4. Cover and cook on low for 6 hours.
5. Stir well and serve.

Nutritional Value (Amount per Serving):

- Calories 477
- Fat 17 g
- Carbohydrates 44 g
- Sugar 7 g
- Protein 41 g
- Cholesterol 116 mg

Vegan White Bean Soup

Preparation Time: 10 minutes   **Cooking Time: 8 hours**   **Serve: 6**

Ingredients:

- 2 cups dry navy beans, soaked overnight & drained
- 1 tsp dried thyme
- ½ tsp dried sage
- ½ tsp dried rosemary
- ½ tsp dried basil
- 6 cups vegetable broth
- 1 tbsp garlic, minced
- 1 medium onion, chopped
- 1 cup celery, chopped
- 1 cup carrots, chopped
- 1 tsp salt

Directions:

1. Add navy beans and remaining ingredients into the slow cooker and stir well.
2. Cover and cook on low for 8 hours.
3. Stir well and serve.

Nutritional Value (Amount per Serving):

- Calories 293
- Fat 2 g
- Carbohydrates 47 g
- Sugar 5 g
- Protein 20 g
- Cholesterol 0 mg

Sweet Potato Chickpea Stew

Preparation Time: 10 minutes   Cooking Time: 4 hours   Serve: 6

Ingredients:

- 30 oz can chickpeas, drained
- 4 cups baby spinach
- 4 cups vegetable broth
- ¼ tsp cinnamon
- 1 tsp ground coriander
- 1 ½ tsp ground cumin
- 1 tsp ground ginger
- 1 tbsp garlic, minced
- 1 lb sweet potatoes, peeled & chopped
- 1 medium onion, chopped
- Pepper
- Salt

Directions:

1. Add all ingredients except spinach into the slow cooker and stir well.
2. Cover and cook on high for 4 hours.
3. Add spinach and stir well.
4. Serve and enjoy.

Nutritional Value (Amount per Serving):

- Calories 301
- Fat 2.9 g
- Carbohydrates 57 g
- Sugar 1.7 g
- Protein 12 g
- Cholesterol 0 mg

Vegan Chickpea Stew

Ingredients:

- 15 oz can chickpeas, drained
- 2 tbsp maple syrup
- 1/8 tsp cayenne pepper
- ½ tsp turmeric
- ½ tsp cinnamon
- 1 tsp paprika
- 2 tsp curry powder
- 1 ½ tsp cumin
- 1 cup vegetable broth
- 2 cups tomato sauce
- 2 potatoes, chopped
- 1 tbsp garlic, minced
- 1 tbsp olive oil
- 1 onion, chopped
- Pepper
- Salt

Directions:

1. Heat oil in a pan over medium-high heat.
2. Add onion and sauté for 3 minutes. Add garlic and sauté for 1 minute.
3. Transfer sautéed onion and remaining ingredients into the slow cooker and stir well.
4. Cover and cook on high for 4 hours.
5. Stir well and serve.

Nutritional Value (Amount per Serving):

- Calories 319
- Fat 5 g
- Carbohydrates 59 g
- Sugar 13 g
- Protein 10 g
- Cholesterol 0 mg

Red Lentil Soup

Ingredients:

- 2 cups dry red lentils
- ¼ tsp pepper
- ¼ tsp chili powder
- 1 tsp dried thyme
- 1 tsp dried basil
- 2 tsp ground cumin
- 1 tbsp lemon juice
- 3 garlic cloves, minced
- 1 onion, diced
- 6 oz tomato paste
- 14 oz can tomatoes
- 3 carrots, chopped
- 6 cups vegetable stock
- Pepper
- Salt

Directions:

1. Add red lentils and remaining ingredients into the slow cooker and stir well.
2. Cover and cook on low for 8 hours.
3. Stir well and serve.

Nutritional Value (Amount per Serving):

- Calories 290
- Fat 1 g
- Carbohydrates 53 g
- Sugar 9 g
- Protein 19 g
- Cholesterol 0 mg

CHAPTER 6: VEGETABLE RECIPES

Balsamic Root Vegetables

Preparation Time: 10 minutes   Cooking Time: 4 hours   Serve: 8

Ingredients:

- 1 ½ lbs sweet potatoes, peeled & cut into 1 ½-inch pieces
- ¾ cup dried cranberries
- 2 onions, chopped
- 1 lb carrots, cut into 1 ½-inch pieces
- 1 lb parsnips, peeled & cut into 1 ½-inch pieces
- 1/3 cup parsley, chopped
- 3 tbsp olive oil
- 2 tbsp balsamic vinegar
- Pepper
- Salt

Directions:

1. Add all ingredients into the slow cooker and stir well.
2. Cover and cook on high for 4 hours.
3. Stir well and serve.

Nutritional Value (Amount per Serving):

- Calories 230
- Fat 5 g
- Carbohydrates 43 g
- Sugar 7 g
- Protein 2 g
- Cholesterol 0 mg

Tomato Compote

Preparation Time: 10 minutes   Cooking Time: 6 hours   Serve: 4

Ingredients:

- 2 lbs cherry tomatoes
- ¼ lemon juice
- ½ tsp red pepper flakes, crushed
- 2 tbsp balsamic vinegar
- 1 tbsp honey
- ½ cup olive oil
- 4 garlic cloves, smashed
- Pepper
- Salt

Directions:

1.Add tomatoes and remaining ingredients into the slow cooker and stir well.
2.Cover and cook on low for 6 hours.
3.Stir well and serve.

Nutritional Value (Amount per Serving):

- Calories 280
- Fat 25 g
- Carbohydrates 14 g
- Sugar 10 g
- Protein 2 g
- Cholesterol 0 mg

Creamy Corn

Preparation Time: 10 minutes   Cooking Time: 3 hours   Serve: 8

Ingredients:

- 2 lbs frozen corn
- ¼ cup chives, sliced
- 8 bacon slices, cooked & crumbled
- 8 oz cream cheese, cut into pieces
- ¼ cup olive oil
- 1 cup milk
- Pepper
- Salt

Directions:

1. Add corn, cream cheese, oil, milk, pepper, and salt into the slow cooker and stir well.
2. Cover and cook on high for 3 hours.
3. Add bacon and chives and stir well.
4. Serve and enjoy.

Nutritional Value (Amount per Serving):

- Calories 202
- Fat 17 g
- Carbohydrates 9 g
- Sugar 2 g
- Protein 4 g
- Cholesterol 34 mg

Cheesy Cauliflower

Preparation Time: 10 minutes   Cooking Time: 3 hours   Serve: 6

Ingredients:

- 1 cauliflower head, cut into florets
- 2 cups cheddar cheese, shredded
- ¼ cup onion, diced
- ½ tsp paprika
- 5 oz can milk
- 1 can condensed cheddar soup
- Pepper
- Salt

Directions:

1. Add cauliflower florets into the slow cooker.
2. Mix together remaining ingredients and pour over cauliflower and stir well.
3. Cover and cook on low for 3 hours.
4. Stir well and serve.

Nutritional Value (Amount per Serving):

- Calories 165
- Fat 12 g
- Carbohydrates 3 g
- Sugar 1 g
- Protein 10 g
- Cholesterol 40 mg

Creamed Corn

Preparation Time: 10 minutes   Cooking Time: 4 hours   Serve: 10

Ingredients:

- 32 oz frozen corn
- ½ tbsp thyme, chopped
- ½ cup milk
- ½ cup olive oil
- 8 oz cream cheese
- Pepper
- Salt

Directions:

1. Add corn and remaining ingredients into the slow cooker and stir well.
2. Cover and cook on low for 4 hours.
3. Stir well and serve.

Nutritional Value (Amount per Serving):

- Calories 594
- Fat 24 g
- Carbohydrates 94 g
- Sugar 16 g
- Protein 18 g
- Cholesterol 26 mg

Artichoke Spinach Dip

Preparation Time: 10 minutes   Cooking Time: 2 hours   Serve: 8

Ingredients:

- 28 oz can artichoke hearts, drained & chopped
- 8 oz cream cheese, cubed
- 1 tbsp red wine vinegar
- 1/3 cup mayonnaise
- ½ cup feta cheese, crumbled
- ¾ cup milk
- ¾ cup parmesan cheese, grated
- 2 garlic cloves, crushed
- 1 small onion, diced
- 1 cup sour cream
- 10 oz frozen spinach, chopped
- Pepper
- Salt

Directions:

1. Add artichoke hearts and remaining ingredients into the slow cooker and stir well.
2. Cover and cook on low for 2 hours.
3. Stir well and serve.

Nutritional Value (Amount per Serving):

- Calories 277
- Fat 21 g
- Carbohydrates 13 g
- Sugar 3.5 g
- Protein 8 g
- Cholesterol 57 mg

Lemon Garlic Asparagus

Preparation Time: 10 minutes   Cooking Time: 2 hours   Serve: 8

Ingredients:

- 30 asparagus spears, rinsed & trimmed
- ¼ tsp red pepper flakes
- 1 tsp basil
- 2 garlic cloves, minced
- ¼ cup water
- ¼ cup lemon juice
- 1 cup water
- 2 lemon slices
- Salt

Directions:

1. Place asparagus spears into the slow cooker.
2. Pour remaining ingredients over asparagus. Cover and cook on low for 2 hours.
3. Serve and enjoy.

Nutritional Value (Amount per Serving):

- Calories 22
- Fat 0.2 g
- Carbohydrates 4 g
- Sugar 1.9 g
- Protein 2.1 g
- Cholesterol 0 mg

Garlic Mushrooms

Preparation Time: 10 minutes   Cooking Time: 3 hours   Serve: 4

Ingredients:

- 2 lbs mushrooms
- 2 tbsp parsley, chopped
- ½ cup olive oil
- 1 tsp Italian seasoning
- 4 garlic cloves, crushed
- Pepper
- Salt

Directions:

1. Add mushrooms, oil, Italian seasoning, garlic, pepper, and salt into the slow cooker and stir well.
2. Cover and cook on low for 3 hours.
3. Garnish with parsley and serve.

Nutritional Value (Amount per Serving):

- Calories 273
- Fat 26 g
- Carbohydrates 8 g
- Sugar 4 g
- Protein 7 g
- Cholesterol 1 mg

Cheesy Squash

Preparation Time: 10 minutes   Cooking Time: 1 hour 30 minutes   Serve: 8

Ingredients:

- 4 medium yellow squash, cut into slices
- 6 oz velveeta cheese, cubed
- 4 tbsp olive oil
- 1 small onion, sliced
- Pepper
- Salt

Directions:

1. Add squash into the slow cooker.
2. Pour remaining ingredients over squash.
3. Cover and cook on low for 1 ½ hours.
4. Serve and enjoy.

Nutritional Value (Amount per Serving):

- Calories 140
- Fat 11 g
- Carbohydrates 6.4 g
- Sugar 3.6 g
- Protein 5 g
- Cholesterol 15 mg

Greek Potatoes

Preparation Time: 10 minutes   Cooking Time: 4 hours   Serve: 8

Ingredients:

- 3 lbs fingerling potatoes, halved
- 2 tbsp parsley, chopped
- 1 lemon zest
- 1 tsp smoked paprika
- 1 tbsp dried oregano
- 4 garlic cloves, minced
- 4 tbsp olive oil
- 1 lemon juice
- Pepper
- Salt

Directions:

1. Add potatoes, paprika, oregano, garlic, oil, lemon juice, pepper, and salt into the slow cooker and stir well.
2. Cover and cook on low for 4 hours.
3. Add lemon zest and parsley and stir well.
4. Serve and enjoy.

Nutritional Value (Amount per Serving):

- Calories 184
- Fat 7 g
- Carbohydrates 28 g
- Sugar 1 g
- Protein 3.4 g
Cholesterol 0 mg

CONCLUSION

The Mediterranean diet is a healthier diet when it is cooked into a slow cooker. The slow cooker is one of the greatest innovations to cook your food with a healthy cooking style. Using the slow cooking method you can cook your food without losing flavors and the nutritional values of the food.

This book contains well-prepared healthy and delicious Mediterranean diet slow cooker recipes that come from different categories like poultry, meat, beans, grains, soups, stews, and vegetables. The recipes written in this cookbook are unique and written in an easily understandable format. All the recipes start with their preparation and exact cooking time followed by step-by-step cooking instructions. The nutritional value information is written at the end of each recipe. The nutritional information will help to keep track of daily calorie intake.

happy cooking

APPENDIX RECIPE INDEX

Made in the USA
Las Vegas, NV
14 November 2023

80766959R00057